A Leisure Arts Publication

*V*ANNA'S CHOICE

Heartfelt Gifts

to Knit & Crochet

Comforting Kids,
One Stitch at a Time

St. Jude patient Andy with Vanna at St. Jude Children's Research Hospital®

LEISURE ARTS, INC.
Little Rock, Arkansas

LION BRAND® YARN COMPANY
New York, New York

St. Jude patient Micah with Vanna

table of CONTENTS

AFGHANS & WRAPS

SLIPPERS

HATS & SCARVES

If you knit or crochet,

the chances are good that you know the happiness of creating handmade gifts. That rewarding feeling is the reason I'm so pleased to be able to introduce this book—*Vanna's Choice Heartfelt Gifts to Knit & Crochet*. Lion Brand® Yarn Company and Leisure Arts have worked together to bring you this new collection of 25 items to create and share with others. You'll find hats, scarves, and wraps that were all knitted or crocheted using a very special yarn.

It's called Vanna's Choice yarn, and it is simply luxurious! One of my favorite features of this soft, premium Lion Brand® yarn is the 23 colors that I chose myself. My goal was to select shades that work together beautifully so that whatever you knit or crochet using Vanna's Choice will be lovely. And because it's an acrylic yarn, it's washable—a nice convenience for everyone!

As you may know, I love to crochet. Whenever I'm not with my family or in front of the camera on Wheel of Fortune, I'm usually working on my latest afghan or scarf. I find that creating gifts for others has a special benefit for me. I not only get the joy of presenting someone with a handmade gift, I get the fun and relaxation of watching my project take shape.

Sharing with others brings up my favorite reason why this new yarn is so important to me. The Lion Brand® Yarn Company supports St. Jude Children's Research Hospital, and so do I. You can rest assured that by using Vanna's Choice yarn, you'll be buying a product from a company with integrity, a company that makes it a priority to give back to those in need.

St. Jude is the charity that's nearest to my heart. I'm fortunate to have two healthy children, Nicholas and Giovanna, but there are so many parents whose children desperately need the healthcare they receive from St. Jude. These quick facts about St. Jude highlight just a few of the reasons why I support this charity.

- St. Jude Children's Research Hospital maintains 60 inpatient beds and treats about 230 patients each day, about 4,900 in active status, most of whom are treated on an outpatient basis.

- It is the first institution established for the sole purpose of conducting basic and clinical research into catastrophic childhood diseases, mainly cancer.

Vanna with St. Jude patients

St. Jude patient Brandon with Vanna

Dr. Michael Dyer in his lab at St. Jude

St. Jude patient Micah with Vanna

"I find that creating **gifts** for others has a special **benefit** for me."

- Research findings at St. Jude are shared with doctors and scientists all over the world.

- Since its inception, St. Jude has developed protocols that have helped to bring survival rates for childhood cancers from less than 20 percent to more than 70 percent overall.

- St. Jude treats children without regard to race, religion, creed or ability to pay.

- St. Jude is the only pediatric research center where families never pay for treatment not covered by insurance, and families without insurance are never asked to pay.

- The late entertainer Danny Thomas founded St. Jude, which opened in 1962.

- The hospital's daily operating costs are primarily covered by public contributions. Their web address is www.stjude.org.

I'm so moved by what this research hospital is doing that I've agreed to be the Hancock Fabrics 2007 Quilt of Dreams spokesperson. In fact, it was through Hancock's fundraising event for St. Jude that I became more fully involved in raising awareness for the hospital.

That was in 2004, and the Quilt of Dreams event included an auction of handmade items to benefit St. Jude. The bidding got off to a slow start and just wasn't picking up momentum as expected. When the auctioneer held up an afghan I had crocheted, I decided to join him onstage to affirm that I did, indeed, create that item, and I pointed out the tag I had attached to it stating that fact. The attendees must have appreciated the additional information, because bidding picked up after that, and I stayed to help show each afghan to the audience.

It was exhilarating for all of us at the event to see St. Jude benefit from our efforts. Once I saw how a little bit of effort can make a big difference, I was hooked on the idea of doing more for St. Jude. That's why I want to encourage you to use Vanna's Choice yarn for all your knitting and crocheting projects, because your hobby can help desperately ill children get the treatments they need!

If you decide to use the knit and crochet patterns in this book to make gifts for charity, I encourage you to first check with hospitals in your area to see if they are needing hats, wraps, or other warm items for their patients. Because of health concerns, most hospitals have guidelines for the submission of handmade items. They may ask for particular items in specific sizes, and they commonly require handmade items to be made of all new, washable materials that haven't been exposed to smoke or pets. Other organizations that may need your skills are shelters, nursing homes, disaster assistance agencies, or non-profit programs such as Warm Up America! or Project Linus. On page 7, you'll find a label that you may photocopy and use to tag your charity gift.

Have fun choosing your favorite patterns from this all-new collection of wraps and accessories. Ultimately—whether you knit or crochet for friends and family or for those in need—passing your handiwork on to others is the nicest gift you can give to yourself.

St. Jude patient Jacob with Vanna

St. Jude patient Miriam with Vanna

"Knowing that your **hobby** is actually **helping** to heal these children is a **great feeling**!"

St. Jude patient Amber with Vanna

We hear it in the news every day. Homes and lives are lost. Violence causes devastation. Misfortune and ill health push individuals to the brink of endurance.

For victims of these and countless other heartbreaking circumstances, there are organizations that can assist with shelter, medical needs, education, and guidance. Many of these charities also distribute garments and blankets. However, these foundations and agencies can't offer help to anyone without first receiving help from donors and volunteers. Whether you can contribute a cap, a scarf, or a blanket, your handmade gift is needed.

To assist you in locating regional and national charities that distribute knitted or crocheted items, the Lion Brand® Yarn Company provides a search feature on their Web site, www.LionBrand.com. At the company's home page, click on *Charity Connection*.

Several national and international organizations that distribute handmade garments and blankets may also have a volunteer chapter in your town. Look up the Web addresses of Newborns in Need, Project Linus, and Warming Families. Warm Up America! is an organization of volunteers sponsored by the Craft Yarn Council of America. These are just a few of the organizations whose work may appeal to you. If you wish to find additional charities in your community, use your favorite search engine to search the words "charity knit crochet" along with the name of your city, county, or parish.

Your telephone directory is another source of charity listings; look under the headings *Crisis Intervention* and *Social Services and Welfare Organizations*. Schools are often aware of families who have clothing needs. Your local police department may collect blankets and toys for children who are removed from dangerous situations. Churches, synagogues, and other religious organizations work with charities and individuals who would benefit from your handiwork. You may even learn that your knowledge of knitting or crochet is valuable in itself—imagine how fulfilling it would be to teach your skill to someone who needs the confidence boost!

You already know how easy it is to create useful items for others. As you can see, it's even simpler to locate a charity that needs your skill. Please give a little time and yarn to help someone else. The talent in your hands can do so much more than just create warmth. It can bring beauty and comfort into the lives of others.

HANDMADE
ESPECIALLY FOR YOU
Size: _____
Fiber Content: _____
_____
Care Instructions: _____
_____
_____

Linen .... #099

White .... #100

Pink .... #101

Navy .... #110

Beige .... #123

Taupe .... #125

Rust .... #135

Dusty Rose .... #140

Rose .... #142

From America's favorite crocheter, Vanna White, comes a specially designed yarn that is soft, washable, and available in a selection of colors that work together beautifully. Use Vanna's Choice yarn for everything from afghans to baby items and accessories—it's a perfect match for the lifestyle of today's busy family.

Silver Blue.................. #105

Dusty Blue.................. #108

Colonial Blue.............. #109

Chocolate.................... #126

Honey .... #130

Brick.............................#133

Antique Rose................ #143

Dusty Purple .... #146

Purple ....#147

Black ....#153

Mustard .... #158

Pea Green ....#170

Dusty Green................ #173

Olive ....#174

AFGHANS & WRAPS

Vanna during her visit to St. Jude

One of the best gifts for someone who's 'on the mend' is a knitted or crocheted afghan. Just imagine snuggling into a soft blanket, knowing that every stitch was made by someone who cares about the challenges you're facing! Starting with this knit wrap in Dusty Purple, you'll find 10 warm afghans—there's a design to suit every age and personality.

—Vanna

knit
CABLE WRAP

◖◼◻◻◻ **EASY +**

Finished Size: 25" x 70" (63.5 x 178 cm)

MATERIALS
    LION BRAND® Vanna's Choice Worsted Weight
      yarn [3.5 ounces, 170 yards (100 grams,
      156 meters) per ball]
      7 balls #146 Dusty Purple
      or color of your choice
    LION BRAND Size 10 [6 mm] knitting needles
    LION BRAND Size 10.5 [6.5 mm] knitting needles or size
      needed for gauge
    LION BRAND cable needle
    LION BRAND stitch markers
    LION BRAND large-eyed blunt needle

MEDIUM 4

GAUGE
8 sts and 24 rows = 4" [10 cm] in Stockinette st
(k on RS, p on WS) using larger needles
BE SURE TO CHECK YOUR GAUGE.

STITCH EXPLANATIONS
2/2 RC (2 over 2 right cross): Slip 2 stitches to cable needle and hold in back, k2, then k2 from cable needle.
4/4 RC (4 over 4 right cross): Slip 4 stitches to cable needle and hold in back, k4, then k4 from cable needle.

PATTERN STITCH
Seed Stitch (over uneven number of stitches)
Row 1: (K1, p1) across to last st, k1.
Rep Row 1 for pattern.

WRAP
With smaller needles, cast on 87 sts.

Rows 1-9: Work in Seed st. Change to larger needles.

Row 10 (Inc Row - RS): Work 5 sts in Seed st, k22, place marker for cable panel, p1, *k1, inc 1 st in next st, k1, p1, (inc 1 st in next st, k1) twice, inc 1 st in next st, p1; rep from * 2 more times, k1, inc 1 st in next st, k1, p1, place marker for cable panel, k22, work last 5 sts in Seed st – 102 sts.

CABLE PANEL

Row 1 (Cable Panel Set Up - WS): Work 5 sts in Seed st, p22, k1, (p4, k1, p8, k1) 3 times, p4, k1, p22, work last 5 sts in Seed st.

Row 2 (RS): Work 5 sts in Seed st, k22, p1, *2/2 RC, p1, 4/4 RC, p1; rep from * 2 more times, 2/2 RC, p1, k22, work last 5 sts in Seed st.

Rows 3, 5 and 7: Work 5 sts in Seed st, p22, k1, *p4, k1, p8, k1; rep from * 2 more times, p4, k1, p22, work last 5 sts in Seed st.

Rows 4 and 8: Work 5 sts in Seed st, k22, p1, *k4, p1, k8, p1; rep from * 2 more times, k4, p1, k22, work last 5 sts in Seed st.

Row 6: Work 5 sts in Seed st, k22, p1, *2/2 RC, p1, k8, p1; rep from * 2 more times, 2/2 RC, p1, k22, work last 5 sts in Seed st.

Row 9: Work 5 sts in Seed st, p22, k1, *p4, k1, p8, k1; rep from * 2 more times, p4, k1, p22, work last 5 sts in Seed st.

Rep Rows 1-9 until piece measures 69" [175.5 cm] from beginning.

Change to smaller needles. Work in Seed st, decreasing 13 sts evenly spaced over cable panel. Work in Seed st for 8 more rows. Bind off in Seed st.

FINISHING
Weave in ends.

crochet
baby LOG CABIN
blanket

◨◨◻◻ EASY +

Finished Size: 36" x 36" (91.5 x 91.5 cm)

MATERIALS

LION BRAND® Vanna's Choice Worsted
Weight yarn [3.5 ounces, 170 yards
(100 grams,156 meters) per ball]
1 ball #101 Pink (A)
1 ball #105 Silver Blue (B)
2 balls #170 Pea Green (C)
2 balls #140 Dusty Rose (D)
3 balls #146 Dusty Purple (E)
or colors of your choice
LION BRAND Size J-10 [6 mm] crochet hook
or size needed for gauge
LION BRAND large-eyed blunt needle

GAUGE

1 Block = 9" [23 cm] square
BE SURE TO CHECK YOUR GAUGE.

NOTE: To change color, work last stitch of first
color until 2 loops remain on hook, yarn over with
next color, draw yarn through 2 loops on hook to
complete stitch.

BLANKET
BLOCK (make 16)
With A, ch 13.

Row 1: Sc in 3rd ch from hook,
*ch 1, skip 1 ch, sc in next ch; rep
from * across.

Row 2: Ch 2, turn, *sc in next ch-1
sp, ch 1; rep from * across to turning
ch, sc in turning ch.

Rows 3-12: Rep Row 2; change to
B in last st of last row.

FIRST BORDER
**Row 1 (worked along top and
side edge of square):** Ch 2, turn,
sc in first ch-1 sp, (ch 1, sc in next
ch-1 sp) 4 times, (ch 1, sc in turning
ch) twice (corner made); turn work
90 degrees to work along side edge;
(ch 1, sc in edge) 6 times evenly
spaced along side edge.

Rows 2-5: Ch 2, turn, sc in first ch-
1 sp, *ch 1, sc in next ch-1 sp; rep
from * across to corner ch-1 sp, (ch
1, sc in corner ch-1 sp) twice, ch 1;
*sc in next ch-1 sp, ch 1; rep from
* across to turning ch, sc in turning
ch; change to C in last st of last row.

SECOND BORDER
Row 1: Turn work 90 degrees to
work along edge of First Border, ch
2, (sc in edge, ch 1) twice evenly
spaced along edge of First Border;
working along opposite side of
foundation ch, sc in first ch-sp, (ch
1, sc in next ch-sp) 4 times evenly
spaced along lower edge, (sc in last
ch-sp, ch 1) twice (corner made);
turn work 90 degrees to work along
last edge of square, (sc in edge, ch
1) 5 times evenly spaced along side
edge; working along edge of First
Border, sc in edge, (ch 1, sc in edge)
twice evenly spaced along edge.

Rows 2-5: Work Rows 2-5 of First Border; change to D in last st of last row.

THIRD BORDER

Row 1: Turn work 90 degrees to work along edge of previous border, ch 2, (sc in edge, ch 1) twice evenly spaced along edge of previous border; (sc in next ch-sp, ch 1) across to corner ch-1 sp, (sc in corner ch-1 sp, ch 1) twice; (sc in ch-1 sp, ch 1) across to other edge of previous border; working along edge of previous border, sc in edge, (ch 1, sc in edge) twice evenly spaced along edge.

Rows 2-5: Work Rows 2-5 of First Border; change to E in last st of last row.

FOURTH BORDER

Rows 1-5: Work as for Third Border. Fasten off.

FINISHING

Arrange squares to form a large square of 4 blocks by 4 blocks. With E, sew squares together.

EDGING

Join E in any corner ch-1 sp, 3 sc in same corner, work (ch 1, sc in next ch-1 sp) around, working 3 sc in each corner; join with sl st in first sc.

Weave in ends.

knit
RIPPLE afghan

⬤⬛⬜⬜ **EASY**

Finished Sizes:
Baby Afghan: 30" x 32½" (76 x 82.5 cm)
Adult Afghan: 38" x 48" (96.5 x 122 cm)

NOTE: Pattern is written for Baby Afghan with changes for Adult Afghan in parentheses. When only one number is given, it applies to both sizes. To follow pattern more easily, circle all numbers pertaining to your size before beginning.

MATERIALS
LION BRAND® Vanna's Choice Worsted Weight
yarn [3.5 ounces, 170 yards (100 grams, 156 meters) per ball]
2 (3) balls #108 Dusty Blue (A)
1 (2) balls #125 Taupe (B)
1 (2) balls #110 Navy (C)
1 (2) balls #099 Linen (D)
1 (2) balls #105 Silver Blue (E)
or colors of your choice
Circular knitting needle size 9 [5.5 mm], 29" [73.5 cm] or size needed for gauge
LION BRAND large-eyed blunt needle

GAUGE
18 sts + 20 rows = 4" [10 cm] in ripple pattern
BE SURE TO CHECK YOUR GAUGE.

COLOR SEQUENCE
*Work 8 rows A, 8 rows B, 8 rows C, 8 rows D, 8 rows E; repeat from * for Color Sequence.

NOTE: Afghan is worked back and forth using circular needle to accommodate large number of sts.

AFGHAN
With A, cast on 126 (162) sts.

Rows 1 and 2: Knit.

Row 3: *(K2tog) 3 times, (increase 1 st in next st) 6 times, (k2tog) 3 times; rep from * to end.

Rows 4-6: Knit.

Row 7: Rep Row 3.

Row 8: Knit. Change to B.

MAIN SECTION
Row 9: Knit.

Row 10: Purl.

Row 11: Rep Row 3.

Row 12: Purl.

Rows 13-16: Rep Rows 9-12. Change to C.

Rep Rows 9-16, working in Color Sequence, for a total of 20 (30) stripes.

Change to A and rep Rows 1-8. With A, knit 1 row. Bind off.

EDGING

From right side with A, pick up and knit 147 (217) sts along one long side of Afghan. Knit 8 rows. Bind off. Rep edging along other long side.

FINISHING

Weave in ends.

knit
STRIPE
afghan

■■□□ **EASY +**

Finished Size: 45" x 55½" (114.5 x 141 cm)

MATERIALS

LION BRAND® Vanna's Choice Worsted Weight
yarn [3½ ounces, 170 yards (100 grams, 156
meters) per ball]
3 balls #110 Navy Blue (A)
3 balls #173 Dusty Green (B)
3 balls #105 Silver Blue (C)
4 balls #108 Dusty Blue (D)
3 balls #170 Pea Green (E)
or colors of your choice
LION BRAND large-eyed blunt needle
Size 9 [5.5 mm] circular knitting needle 36"
[91.5 cm] long or size needed for gauge

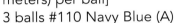 **MEDIUM 4**

GAUGE

16 sts and 32 rows = 4" [10 cm] in Garter st (k every row).

NOTE: Circular needle is used to accommodate large number of
stitches. Work back and forth on circular needle as if working on
straight needles.

COLOR SEQUENCES

Strip 1: *Work 20 rows each of A, B, C, D, E; rep from * for Strip 1.
Strip 2: *Work 20 rows each of B, C, D, E, A; rep from * for Strip 2.
Strip 3: *Work 20 rows each of C, D, E, A, B; rep from * for Strip 3.
Strip 4: *Work 20 rows each of D, E, A, B, C; rep from * for Strip 4.

AFGHAN
DIAGONAL STRIP (make one each of Strip 1, 2, 3, and 4)
LOWER SECTION

With first color in Color Sequence,
cast on 1 st.
Row 1 (RS): K into front, back and
front of stitch – 3 sts.
Row 2 and All WS Rows: Knit.
Row 3: Inc 1 in first st, k1, inc 1 in
last st – 5 sts.
Row 5: Inc 1 in first st, k to last st,
inc 1 in last st – 7 sts.
Continue to inc 1 st in first and last
st of every other row until there are
21 sts.
Change to next color in Color
Sequence and continue to inc 1 st
in first and last st of every other row
until there are 41 sts.
Change to next color in Color
Sequence and continue to inc 1 st
in first and last st of every other row
until there are 61 sts.

CENTER SECTION

Continue in Color Sequence as
established.
Row 1 (RS): Inc 1 st in first st, k to
last 2 sts, k2 tog – 61 sts.
Row 2 and All WS Rows: Knit.
Rep last 2 rows, continuing in
Color Sequence and changing colors
every 20 rows until 3 reps of Color
Sequence have been worked.

TOP SECTION

Continue in Color Sequence as
established.
Row 1: K2 tog, k to last 2 sts, k2
tog – 59 sts.
Row 2 and All WS Rows: Knit.
Rep last 2 rows, following Color
Sequence and changing colors every
20 rows until 3 sts remain.
Last Row: K3tog – 1 st.
Fasten off.

FINISHING

Beginning with Strip 1, sew strips together in numerical order.

TOP EDGING

From RS, with A, pick up and k 156 sts along top edge. Knit 1 row. Change to D. Knit 8 rows, inc 1 st at each end of every RS row. Change to A. Knit 1 row, inc 1 st at each end. Bind off.

LOWER EDGING

Work as for Top Edging.

SIDE EDGING

From RS, with A, pick up and k 194 sts along side edge. Work as for Top Edging. Rep on opposite side of Afghan.

Seam edging at corners. Weave in ends.

crochet
GRANNY SQUARE
wrap

■■□□ EASY

Finished Size: 25" x 70" (63.5 x 178 cm)

MATERIALS
LION BRAND® Vanna's Choice Worsted **4** MEDIUM
Weight yarn [3.5 ounces, 170 yards
(100 grams, 156 meters) per ball]
3 balls #126 Chocolate (A)
3 balls #142 Rose (B)
3 balls #140 Dusty Rose (C)
3 balls #101 Pink (D)
or colors of your choice
LION BRAND Size J-10 [6 mm] crochet hook
or size needed for gauge
LION BRAND large-eyed blunt needle

GAUGE
1 Granny Square = 5" x 5" [12.5 x 12.5 cm]
BE SURE TO CHECK YOUR GAUGE.

WRAP
GRANNY SQUARE I
(make 35)
With A, ch 3; join with sl st in first ch to form a ring.

Rnd 1: Ch 3, 2 dc in ring, ch 2, (3 dc in ring, ch 2) 3 times; join with sl st in top of beg ch. Fasten off A.

Rnd 2: Join B with sl st in any ch-2 sp. Ch 3, (2 dc, ch 2, 3 dc) in same sp, ch 1, *(3 dc, ch 2, 3 dc) in next ch-2 sp, ch 1; rep from * 2 more times; join with sl st in top of beg ch. Fasten off B.

Rnd 3: Join C with sl st in any ch-2 sp. Ch 3, (2 dc, ch 2, 3 dc) in same sp, ch 1, 3 dc in next ch-1 sp, ch 1, *(3 dc, ch 2, 3 dc) in next ch-2 sp, ch 1, 3 dc in next ch-1 sp, ch 1; rep from * 2 more times; join with sl st in top of beg ch. Fasten off C.

Rnd 4: Join D with sl st in any ch-2 sp. Ch 3, (2 dc, ch 2, 3 dc) in same sp, ch 1, (3 dc in next ch-1 sp, ch 1) twice, *(3 dc, ch 2, 3 dc) in next ch-2 sp, ch 1, (3 dc in next ch-1 sp, ch 1) twice; rep from * 2 more times; join with sl st in top of beg ch. Fasten off D.

GRANNY SQUARE II
(make 35)
With D, ch 3; join with sl st in first ch to form a ring. Work as for Square 1, changing colors every rnd and working color sequence as follows: D, C, B, A.

FINISHING

Sew squares together in 5 strips of 14 squares each, alternating Granny Square I and Granny Square II. Begin 3 strips with Granny Square I. Begin 2 strips with Granny Square II. Sew strips together.

EDGING

From right side, join A with sl st in any corner ch-2 sp.

Rnd 1: Ch 1, work 3 sc in same ch-2 sp, sc in each dc and ch-1 sp around, working 3 sc in each corner ch-2 sp; join with sl st in first sc. Fasten off.

Weave in ends.

◖◼◻◻ **EASY +**

Finished Size: 34" x 34" (86.5 x 86.5 cm)

MATERIALS
LION BRAND® Vanna's Choice Worsted Weight
yarn [3.5 ounces, 170 yards (100 grams,
156 meters) per ball]
4 balls #153 Black (A)
2 balls #099 Linen (B)
2 balls #133 Brick (C)
or colors of your choice
LION BRAND stitch holders
LION BRAND large-eyed blunt needle
Size 9 [5.5 mm] circular knitting needle, 32" [81.5 cm] or
size needed for gauge

GAUGE
16 sts and 32 rows = 4" [10 cm] in Garter st
(k every row)
BE SURE TO CHECK YOUR GAUGE.

NOTES:
1) Squares are worked in intarsia. Use a separate strand or
ball of yarn for each color. Twist yarns around each other
when changing colors to prevent holes.
2) Circular needle is used to accommodate large number
of edging stitches. Work back and forth in rows on circular
needle, as if working on straight needles.

knit
GRAPHIC
BLOCK
afghan

AFGHAN
STRIP A (make 3)
With A, cast on 26 sts.

*Working back and forth on circular
needle, knit 52 rows.

Change to B.

Rows 1-8: With B, knit.

Rows 9-16: With B, k4; with A,
k18; with B, k4.

Rows 17-36: With B, k4; with A,
k4; with C, k10; with A, k4; with B,
k4.

Rows 37-44: Rep Rows 9-16.

Rows 45-52: Rep Rows 1-8.

Rep from * once more.

With A, knit 52 rows. Slip stitches
to a stitch holder.

STRIP B (make 2)
With B, cast on 26 sts.

* Rows 1-8: With B, knit.

Rows 9-16: With B, k4; with C, k18; with B, k4.

Rows 17-36: With B, k4; with C, k4; with A, k10; with C, k4; with B, k4.

Rows 37-44: Rep Rows 9-16.

Rows 45-52: Rep Rows 1-8.

With A, knit 52 rows.

Rep from * once more.

Rep Rows 1-52. Slip stitches to a stitch holder.

FINISHING
Beginning and ending with a Strip A, and alternating strips A and B, sew strips together.

EDGING
With C, k across 26 sts from each holder – 130 sts.

Knit 6 rows. Bind off.

With C, pick up and k 26 sts along cast-on edge of each strip – 130 sts.

Knit 6 rows. Bind off.

SIDE EDGINGS
With C, pick up and k 4 sts along end of edging, 27 sts along side of each color block, k 4 sts along side of edging – 143 sts.

Knit 6 rows. Bind off.

Rep edging along opposite side of Afghan.

Weave in ends.

knit
SAW TOOTH EDGE afghan

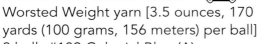 **EASY**

Finished Size: 27" x 32" (68.5 x 81.5 cm)

MATERIALS

LION BRAND® Vanna's Choice
Worsted Weight yarn [3.5 ounces, 170
yards (100 grams, 156 meters) per ball]
2 balls #109 Colonial Blue (A)
2 balls #123 Beige (B)
1 ball #174 Olive (C)
1 ball #133 Brick (D)
1 ball #158 Mustard (E)
1 ball #135 Rust (F)
or colors of your choice
LION BRAND Size 9 [5.5 mm] knitting
needles or size needed for gauge
LION BRAND large-eyed blunt needle

GAUGE

16 sts and 32 rows = 4" [10 cm] in Garter st
(k every row)
BE SURE TO CHECK YOUR GAUGE.

AFGHAN

With A, cast on 100 sts.

Rows 1 and 2: With A, knit.

Rows 3 and 4: With B, knit.

Rows 5 and 6: With A, knit.

Rep Rows 3-6 until there are a
total of 238 rows (119 ridges).
Do not bind off.

SAW TOOTH EDGING

With C, k10, turn and work
on these 10 sts only.

Row 1: K2tog, k6, k2tog.

Row 2: K8.

Row 3: k2tog, k4, k2tog.

Row 4: K6.

Row 5: k2tog, k2, k2tog.

Row 6: K4.

Row 7: (K2tog) twice.

Row 8: K2tog. Fasten off.

With D, k next 10 sts and rep
Rows 1-8.

Continue to work Saw Tooth
Edging over 10 sts in the
following Color Sequence: *E,
F, C, D; rep from * across row
(for a total of 10 Saw Tooth
reps).

Continuing in Color
Sequence, pick up and k 10
sts along side edge of Afghan.
Work Saw Tooth Edging 12
times along side edge.

Continuing in Color
Sequence, pick up and k 10 sts
along cast-on edge. Work Saw
Tooth Edging 10 times along
cast-on edge.

Continuing in Color
Sequence, work Saw Tooth
edging along remaining side
12 times, ending with F (for a
total of 44 Saw Tooth reps).

FINISHING
Weave in ends.

From left: St. Jude patients Andy, Sebastien, Micah, Ke'Von & Amber

I recently had the joy of presenting a check from Wheel of Fortune and Country Music Stars to David L. McKee, Chief Operating Officer of ALSAC/St. Jude. I can't say enough good things about the work done at St. Jude!

—Vanna

crochet
SAW TOOTH
SQUARES
afghan

Finished Size: 36" x 40"
(91.5 x 101.5 cm)

MATERIALS
LION BRAND®
Vanna's Choice Worsted
Weight yarn [3.5 ounces, 170
yards (100 grams, 156 meters)
per ball]
4 balls #133 Brick (A)
3 balls #130 Honey (B)
or colors of your choice
LION BRAND Size J-10 [6 mm]
crochet hook or size needed
for gauge
LION BRAND large-eyed blunt
needle

GAUGE
12 hdc and 6½ rows = 4"[10 cm]
BE SURE TO CHECK YOUR
GAUGE.

NOTE: To change color, work last
stitch of first color until 3 loops
remain on hook, yarn over with
next color, draw yarn through 3
loops on hook. Carry color not in
use loosely along tops of stitches
and work over carried yarn to
hide.

AFGHAN
SQUARE 1 (make 6)
With A, ch 30.

Row 1: Hdc in 3rd ch from hook
and each ch across – 28 hdc.

Rows 2 and 3: Ch 2, turn, hdc in
each hdc across; change to B in last
st of last row.

Begin Saw Tooth Pattern
Row 1: With B, ch 2, turn, hdc in
first 4 hdc; change to A, hdc in last
24 hdc.

Row 2: With A, ch 2, turn, hdc in
first 24 hdc; change to B, hdc in last
4 hdc.

Row 3: Rep Row 1.

Row 4 (Second Saw Tooth): With
A, ch 2, turn, hdc in first 20 hdc;
change to B, hdc in last 8 hdc.

Row 5: With B, ch 2, turn, hdc in
first 8 hdc, change to A, hdc in last
20 hdc.

Row 6: Rep Row 4.

Row 7 (Third Saw Tooth): With
B, ch 2, turn, hdc in first 12 hdc;
change to A, hdc in last 16 hdc.

Row 8: With A, ch 2, turn, hdc in
first 16 hdc, change to B, hdc in last
12 hdc.

Row 9: Rep Row 7.

Row 10 (Fourth Saw Tooth): With
A, ch 2, turn, hdc in first 12 hdc;
change to B, hdc in last 16 hdc.

Row 11: With B, ch 2, turn, hdc in
first 16 hdc; change to A, hdc in last
12 hdc.

Row 12: Rep Row 10.

Row 13 (Fifth Saw Tooth): With
B, ch 2, turn, hdc in first 20 hdc;
change to A, hdc in last 8 hdc.

Row 14: With A, ch 2, turn, hdc in first 8 hdc; change to B, hdc in last 20 hdc.

Row 15: Rep Row 13.

Row 16 (Sixth Saw Tooth): With A, ch 2, turn, hdc in first 4 hdc; change to B, hdc in last 24 hdc.

Row 17: With B, ch 2, turn, hdc in first 24 hdc; change to A, hdc in last 4 hdc.

Row 18: Rep Row 16. Fasten off.

SQUARE 2 (make 6)
Work as for Square 1, reversing colors by using A for B and B for A.

FINISHING
STRIP A (make 2)
Sew 4 squares as follows: 1, 2, 1, 2 to make Strip A.

STRIP B (make 1)
Sew 4 squares as follows: 2, 1, 2, 1 to make Strip B.
Sew a Strip A to each side of Strip B.

EDGING
From RS, join A with slip stitch in any corner.

Rnd 1: *Work 3 sc in corner, work sc evenly spaced across to next corner; rep from * around; join with sl st in first sc.

Rnds 2 and 3: Ch 1, sc in each sc around, working 3 sc in center sc of each corner.

Fasten off.
Weave in ends.

crochet TEEN'S
lap afghan

◼◼◻◻ **EASY**

Finished Size: 36" x 48" (91.5 x 122 cm)

MATERIALS

LION BRAND® Vanna's Choice Worsted **MEDIUM 4**
  Weight yarn [3.5 ounces, 170 yards (100 grams,
  156 meters) per ball]
  2 balls #109 Colonial Blue (A)
  2 balls #135 Rust (B)
  2 balls #108 Dusty Blue (C)
  3 balls #110 Navy (D)
  or colors of your choice
LION BRAND Size J-10 [6 mm] crochet hook or size
  needed for gauge
LION BRAND Pom Pom maker
LION BRAND large-eyed blunt needle

GAUGE

11 hdc and 8½ rows = 4" [10 cm]
BE SURE TO CHECK YOUR GAUGE.

COLOR SEQUENCE

*Work 2 rows with A, 2 rows with B, 2 rows with C, 2
rows with D; rep from * for Color Sequence.

NOTE: To change color, work last stitch of first color
until 3 loops remain on hook, yarn over with next color,
draw yarn through all 3 loops on hook to complete
stitch.

AFGHAN

With A, ch 101.

Row 1: Hdc in 3rd ch from hook
and each ch across – 99 hdc.

Row 2: Ch 2, turn, hdc in each hdc
across; change to B in last st.

Following Color Sequence, rep Row
2, working 2 rows of each color. Rep
Color Sequence a total of 12 times
(for a total of 96 rows). Then work
2 rows each with A, B, and C (for a
total of 102 rows), changing to D in
the last st.

EDGING

Rnd 1: With D, work sc evenly
spaced around entire afghan,
working 3 sc in each corner; join
with sl st in first sc.

Rnd 2: Ch 1, turn, sc in each sc
around, working 3 sc in center sc of
each corner; join with sl st in first sc.
Fasten off.

FINISHING
POM POM (make 4 each with
A, B, C and D)
Follow package instructions to make
large pom poms. Securely fasten
one pom pom of each color to each
corner of Afghan.

Weave in ends.

crochet
SECURITY
blanket

■■□□ EASY

Finished Size: 24" x 37" (61 x 94 cm)

MATERIALS

LION BRAND® Vanna's Choice [MEDIUM 4]
Worsted Weight yarn [3.5 ounces,
170 yards (100 grams, 156 meters)
per ball]
2 balls #105 Silver Blue (A)
2 balls #123 Beige (B)
2 balls #101 Pink (C)
or colors of your choice
LION BRAND Size J-10 [6 mm]
crochet hook or size needed for
gauge
LION BRAND large-eyed blunt
needle
4" [10 cm] piece of heavy cardboard

GAUGE

11 hdc and 8½ rows = 4" [10 cm]
BE SURE TO CHECK YOUR GAUGE.

COLOR SEQUENCE

*Work 2 rows with A, 2 rows with B,
2 rows with C; rep from * for Color
Sequence.

Note: To change color, work last stitch of first color until 3 loops remain on hook, yarn over with next color, draw yarn through all 3 loops on hook to complete stitch.

BLANKET

With A, ch 68.

Row 1: Hdc in 3rd ch from hook and each ch across – 66 hdc.

Row 2: Ch 2, turn, hdc in each hdc across; change to B in last st.

Following Color Sequence, rep Row 2, working 2 rows of each color. Rep Color Sequence a total of 13 times (for a total of 78 rows), changing to B in the last st.

EDGING

Rnd 1: With B, work sc evenly spaced around entire afghan, working sc in each corner; join with sl st in first sc.

Rnd 2: Ch 1, turn, sc in each sc around, working 3 sc in center sc of each corner; join with sl st in first sc.

Fasten off.

FINISHING
TASSEL (make 4)

Holding 1 strand each of A, B and C together, wrap yarn around 4" [1 cm] piece of heavy cardboard 10 times. Cut a 6" [15 cm] length of B and thread onto large-eyed blunt needle. Insert needle under all strand at upper edge of cardboard. Pull tightly and knot securely near strands Cut yarn loops at lower edge of cardboard. Cut an 8" [20.5 cm] length of B and wrap tightly around loops 1" [2.5 cm] below top knot to for Tassel neck. Knot securely; thread ends onto needle and weave ends to center of Tassel. Trim Tassel ends evenly.

Sew a Tassel to each corner of Blanket.

Weave in ends.

crochet
SAMPLER
afghan

◨■▢▢ EASY +

Finished Size: 36" x 46½" (91.5 x 118 cm)

MATERIALS
LION BRAND® Vanna's Choice Worsted
Weight yarn [3.5 ounces,
170 yards (100 grams, 156
meters) per ball]

MEDIUM 4

4 balls #108 Dusty Blue (A)
2 balls #158 Mustard (B)
2 balls #135 Rust (C)
2 balls #170 Pea Green (D)
or colors of your choice
LION BRAND Size J-10 [6 mm] crochet
hook or size needed for gauge
LION BRAND large-eyed blunt needle

GAUGE
1 Block = 8" x 8½" [20.5 x 21.5 cm]
BE SURE TO CHECK YOUR GAUGE.

STITCH EXPLANATION
Popcorn (PC): 4 dc in same stitch, remove
hook from work and insert in first dc of 4-dc
group, pick up loop of last dc of 4-dc group,
and pull through to close, ch 1.

AFGHAN
BLOCK I (make 5)
With A, ch 22.

Row 1: Sc in 2nd ch from hook and each
ch across – 21 sc.

Row 2: Ch 3, turn, sk first sc, PC in
next sc, (dc in next 3 sc, PC in next sc) 4
times, dc in last 3 sc.

Row 3: Ch 1, turn, sc in first 3 dc, sc in
top of PC, (sc in next 3 dc, sc in top of
PC) 4 times, sc in top of turning ch.

Row 4: Ch 3, turn, sk first sc, dc in next
2 sc, (PC in next sc, dc in next 3 sc) 4
times, PC in next sc, dc in last sc.

Row 5: Ch 1, turn, sc in first dc, (sc in
top of PC, sc in next 3 dc) 4 times, sc in
top of PC, sc in next 2 dc, sc in top of
turning ch.

Rows 6-17: Rep last 4 rows 3 times.

Rows 18 and 19: Rep Rows 2 and 3.

Row 20: Ch 1, turn, sc evenly spaced
around entire square, working 3 sc in
each corner; join with sl st in first sc.

Fasten off.

Since playtime is such an important part of childhood, St. Jude provides playrooms and toys for their young patients. One little boy thought of a new use for Vanna's Choice Yarn—the toys needed scarves!
—Vanna

Whenever I visit St. Jude Children's Research Hospital, I meet the most wonderful young people, like St. Jude patient Carey. They inspire me with their courage and their dreams. They make me want to do more for them and for others who need help and hope.

—Vanna

BLOCK II (make 5)
With B, ch 24.

Row 1: Dc in 4th ch from hook, dc in next 2 ch, *sk next 2 ch, (2 dc, ch 2, 2 dc) in next ch (shell made), sk 2 ch, dc in next 4 ch; rep from * across – 2 shells.

Row 2: Ch 3, turn, sk first dc, dc in next 3 dc, *ch 2, sk first 2 dc of shell, (sc, ch 3, sc) in ch-2 sp of shell, ch 2, sk last 2 dc of shell, dc in next 4 dc; rep from * across working last dc of last rep in top of turning ch.

Row 3: Ch 3, turn, sk first dc, dc in next 3 dc, *sk 1 sc, shell in next ch-3 sp, sk 1 sc, dc in next 4 dc; rep from * across working last dc of last rep in top of turning ch.

Rows 4-13: Rep last 2 rows 5 times.

Row 14: Ch 3, turn, sk first dc, dc in next 3 dc, *hdc in next 2 dc, sc in next ch-2 sp, hdc in next 2 dc, dc in next 4 dc; rep from * across working last dc of last rep in top of turning ch.

Row 15: Ch 1, turn, sc evenly around entire square, working 3 sc in each corner; join with sl st in first sc.

Row 16: Ch 1, sc in each sc around, working 3 sc in each corner; join with sl st in first sc.

Fasten off.

BLOCK III (make 5)
With C, ch 27.

Row 1: Dc in 7th ch from hook, (dc, ch 3, 2 dc) in same ch (shell made), *sk 3 ch, (dc, ch 2, dc) in next ch (V-st made), sk 3 ch, (2 dc, ch 3, 2 dc) in next ch (shell made); rep from * to last 4 ch, sk 3 ch, dc in last ch – 3 shells.

Rows 2-10: Ch 3, turn, shell in ch-3 sp of first shell, *V-st in ch-2 sp of next V-st, shell in ch-3 sp of next shell; rep from * across, dc in top of turning ch.

Row 11: Ch 5, turn, sc in ch-3 sp of first shell, *ch 2, V-st in ch-2 sp of next V-st, ch 2, sc in ch-3 sp of next shell; rep from * across, ch 2, dc in top of turning ch.

Rnd 12: Ch 1, turn, sc evenly spaced around entire square, working 3 sc in each corner; join with sl st in first sc.

Rnd 13: Ch 1, sc in each sc around, working 3 sc in each corner; join with sl st in first sc.

Fasten off.

BLOCK IV (make 5)
With D, ch 20.

Row 1 (RS): Sc in 2nd ch from hook and each ch across — 19 sc.

Row 2: Ch 1, turn, sc in first sc, *ch 7, sk 5 sc, sc in next sc; rep from * across.

Row 3: Ch 1, turn, sc in first sc, *holding ch-7 loop in front of work, sc in next 5 sc of previous row, sc in next sc; rep from * across.

Row 4: Ch 1, turn, sc in each sc across.

Row 5: Ch 1, turn, sc in first 3 sc, (slipping hook under ch-7 loop to catch loop, sc in next sc, sc in next 5 sc) twice, slipping hook under ch-7 loop to catch, sc in next sc, sc in last 3 sc.

Row 6: Ch 1, turn, sc in first sc, ch 5, sk 2 sc, (sc in next sc, ch 7, sk 5 sc) twice, sc in next sc, ch 5, sk 2 sc, sc in last sc.

Row 7: Ch 1, turn, sc in first sc, holding ch-5 loop in front of work, sc in next 2 sc of previous row, sc in next sc, (holding ch-7 loop in front of work, sc in next 5 sc of previous row, sc in next sc) twice, holding ch-5 loop in front of work, sc in next 2 sc of previous row, sc in last sc.

Row 8: Ch 1, turn, sc in each sc across.

Row 9: Ch 1, turn, slipping hook under ch-5 loop to catch loop, sc in first sc, (sc in next 5 sc, slipping hook under ch-7 loop to catch, sc in next sc) twice, sc in next 5 sc, slipping hook under ch-5 loop to catch, sc in last sc.

Rows 10-25: Rep Rows 2-9 twice.

Rows 26-29: Rep Rows 2-5.

Rnd 30: Ch 1, turn, sc evenly spaced around entire square, working 3 sc in each corner; join with sl st in first sc.

Rnds 31 and 32: Ch 1, sc in each sc around, working 3 sc in each corner; join with sl st in first sc.

Fasten off.

FINISHING
Following Assembly Diagram, sew blocks together.

BORDER
From RS, join A with sl st in any corner.

Rnd 1: Ch 1, sc evenly spaced around entire afghan, working 3 sc in each corner; join with sl st in first sc.

Rnds 2-8: Ch 1, sc in each sc around, working 3 sc in each corner; join with sl st in first sc.

Fasten off.

Weave in ends.

ASSEMBLY DIAGRAM

II	I	III	IV
IV	III	I	II
II	I	III	IV
IV	III	I	II
II	I	III	IV

SLIPPERS

St. Jude patient Kelly with Vanna

Hospitals and other healthcare facilities have to be kept cool to encourage a germ-free environment. On the next few pages, you'll find five patterns for slippers that can help patients chase the chill. These particular loafer-style slippers are made in standard sizes for women.

—Vanna

crochet
LOAFER
slippers

◼◼◻◻ **EASY**

Finished Sizes: Adult S (M, L)
Foot Length: 8 (9, 10)" [20.5 (23, 25.5) cm]

NOTE: Pattern is written for smallest size with changes for larger sizes in parentheses. When only one number is given, it applies to all sizes. To follow pattern more easily, circle all numbers pertaining to your size before beginning.

MATERIALS
LION BRAND® Vanna's Choice Worsted
Weight yarn [3.5 ounces, 170 yards
(100 grams, 156 meters) per ball]
1 ball #133 Brick (A)
1 ball #170 Pea Green (B)
or colors of your choice
LION BRAND Size K-10.5 [6.5 mm] crochet hook or size needed for gauge
LION BRAND split ring markers
LION BRAND large-eyed blunt needle

MEDIUM 4

GAUGE
12 sc and 16 rows = 4" [10 cm]
BE SURE TO CHECK YOUR GAUGE.

NOTE: Markers are used to indicate placement of toe and heel. Move markers up each round.

SLIPPERS
SOLE (make 2)
With A, ch 16 (18, 20).

Rnd 1: Sc in 2nd ch from hook and in each ch to last ch, work 3 sc in last ch. Mark center of 3 sc for toe. Working along opposite side of foundation ch, sc in each ch to last ch, 2 sc in last ch (same ch as first sc), mark 2nd sc for heel and beg of rnd; join with sl st in first sc – 32 (36, 40) sc.

Rnds 2-4: Ch 1, sc in each sc around, working 3 sc in marked sc of toe and heel; join with sl st in first sc – 44 (48, 52) sc.

Rnd 5: Ch 1, sc in each sc to 3 center sc of toe, 2 sc in each of these 3 sc, sc in each sc to center 3 sc of heel, 2 sc in next sc, sc in next sc, sc in same sc as first sc; join with sl st in first sc – 49 (53, 57) sc.
Mark center of each side of sole.

Rnd 6: Ch 1, sc in each sc to first side marker, hdc in each sc to next side marker, sc in each sc around; join with sl st in first sc to join. Fasten off A.

UPPER

Join B with sl st in same space.

Rnd 1: Ch 2 (counts as first hdc), hdc in back loop of each sc around; join with sl st in top of beg ch.

Rnds 2 and 3: Ch 2, hdc in each hdc around; join with sl st in top of beg ch. Fasten off.

INSTEP (make 2)
With B, ch 5.

Row 1: Sc in 2nd ch from hook and each ch across – 4 sc.

Row 2: Ch 1, turn, 2 sc in first sc, sc in each sc across to last sc, 2 sc in last sc – 6 sc.

Row 3: Ch 1, turn, sc in each sc across.

Rows 4-7: Rep Rows 2 and 3 – 10 sc.

Rep Row 3 until piece measures $3^1/2$ (4, $4^1/2$)" [9 (10, 11.5) cm] from beg.

Next Row: Ch 1, sk first sc, sc in each sc across. Rep last row until 6 sc remain. Fasten off.

FINISHING

Pin Instep into Upper with shaped end of Instep at toe. From RS, with A and working through both thicknesses, sc evenly around edge to join; working through Instep only, sc evenly across top edge of Instep. Do not fasten off.

TIE CASING
Continuing with A, sl st into top edge of Slipper, close to edge of Upper.

Row 1: Ch 1, sc in each hdc around Slipper opening, ending close to opposite side of Upper.

Rows 2-5: Ch 1, turn, sc in each sc across. Fasten off. Fold casing in half to RS and sew in place.

TIES (make 2)
With A, make a ch about 20" [51 cm] long. Weave ch through casing, bringing ends of ch through from inside of Slipper to RS at center front of Upper.

Weave in ends.

crochet
POM POM
slippers

■■□□ EASY

Finished Sizes: Child's S (M, L)
Foot Length: 5 (6, 7)" [12.5 (15, 18) cm]

NOTE: Pattern is written for smallest size with changes for larger sizes in parentheses. When only one number is given, it applies to all sizes. To follow pattern more easily, circle all numbers pertaining to your size before beginning.

MATERIALS
LION BRAND® Vanna's Choice Worsted Weight
  yarn [3.5 ounces, 170 yards
  (100 grams, 156 meters) per ball]
  1 ball #108 Dusty Blue (A)
  1 ball #170 Pea Green (B)
  or colors of your choice
LION BRAND Size K-10.5 [6.5 mm] crochet hook or
  size needed for gauge
LION BRAND split ring markers
LION BRAND Pom Pom maker
LION BRAND large-eyed blunt needle

GAUGE
12 sc and 16 rows = 4" [10 cm]
BE SURE TO CHECK YOUR GAUGE.

NOTE: Markers are used to indicate placement of toe and heel. Move markers up each round.

SLIPPERS
SOLE (make 2)
With A, ch 10 (12, 14).

Rnd 1: Sc in 2nd ch from hook and in each ch to last ch, work 3 sc in last ch. Mark center of 3 sc for toe. Working along opposite side of foundation ch, sc in each ch to last ch, 2 sc in last ch (same ch as first sc), mark 2nd sc for heel and beg of rnd; join with sl st in first sc – 20 (24, 28) sc.

Rnds 2-3 (3, 4): Ch 1, sc in each sc around, working 3 sc in marked sc of toe and heel; join with sl st in first sc – 28 (32, 40) sc.

Rnd 4 (4, 5): Ch 1, sc in each sc to 3 center sc of toe, 2 sc in each of next 3 sc, sc in each sc to center 3 sc of heel, 2 sc in next sc, sc in next sc, sc in same sc as first sc; join with sl st in first sc – 33 (37, 45) sc.

Mark center of each side of sole.

Rnd 5 (5, 6): Ch 1, sc in each sc to first side marker, hdc in each sc to next side marker, sc in each sc around; join with sl st in first sc to join.

Rnd 6 (6, 7): Ch 1, sc in back loop of each sc around; join with sl st in first sc. Fasten off.

UPPER

Join B with sl st in first sc.

Rnd 1: Ch 2, hdc in each sc around; join with sl st in top of beg ch.

Rnds 2 and 3: Ch 2, hdc in each hdc to 1 st before toe marker, sk 1 st, hdc in marked st, sk next st, hdc in each hdc around; join with sl st in top of beg ch.

Rnds 4-5 (6, 6): Ch 2, hdc in each hdc to 5 sts before toe marker, (sk 1 st, hdc in next st) twice, sk 1 st, hdc in marked toe st, (skip 1 st, hdc in next st) twice, sk 1 st, hdc in each hdc around; join with sl st in top of beg ch.

Rnd 6 (7, 7): Ch 2, hdc in each hdc around; join with sl st in top of beg ch.

Repeat Rnd 6 (7, 7) for 3 (3½, 4)" [7.5 (9, 10) cm]. Fasten off.

Last Rnd: Join A with sl st in first hdc, ch 1, sc in each hdc around; join with sl st in first st.

Fasten off.

FINISHING
POM POM (make 2)

Following package instructions, with A and B held together make 2 small pom poms. Trim ends. Sew a pom pom to each Slipper.

Weave in ends.

crochet **FLOWER** slippers

◼◼▭▭ **EASY**

Finished Sizes: 3-9 (9-12, 12-24) months
Foot Length: 3 (3½, 4)" [7.5 (9, 10) cm]

NOTE: Pattern is written for smallest size with changes for larger sizes in parentheses. When only one number is given, it applies to all sizes. To follow pattern more easily, circle all numbers pertaining to your size before beginning.

MATERIALS

MEDIUM 4

LION BRAND® Vanna's Choice Worsted Weight yarn [3.5 ounces, 170 yards (100 grams, 156 meters) per ball]
1 ball #170 Pea Green (A)
1 ball #142 Rose (B)
1 ball #101 Pink (C)
or colors of your choice
LION BRAND Size K-10.5 [6.5 mm] crochet hook or size needed for gauge
LION BRAND split ring markers
LION BRAND large-eyed blunt needle

GAUGE

12 sc and 16 rows = 4" [10 cm]
BE SURE TO CHECK YOUR GAUGE.

SLIPPERS
SOLE (make 2)
With A, ch 4 (6, 8).

Rnd 1: Sc in 2nd ch from hook and each ch across to last ch, 3 sc in last ch, mark center of 3 sc for toe; working along opposite side of foundation ch, sc in each ch to last ch, 2 sc in last ch (same ch as first sc), mark 2nd sc for heel and beginning of rnd; join with sl st in first sc – 8 (12, 16) sc. Move markers up each rnd.

Rnd 2: Ch 1, sc in each sc around, working 3 sc in marked sc of toe and heel; join with sl st in first sc – 12 (16, 20) sc.

Rnd 3: Ch 1, sc in each sc to 3 center sc of toe, 2 sc in each of these 3 sc, sc in each sc to center 3 sc of heel, 2 sc in next sc, sc in next sc, sc in same sc as first sc; join with sl st in first sc – 17 (21, 25) sc.

Mark center along each side of sole.

Rnd 4: Ch 1, sc in each sc to first side marker, hdc in each sc to next side marker, sc in each sc around; join with sl st in first sc.

Rnd 5: Ch 1, sc in back loop of each sc around; join with sl st in first sc. Fasten off.

UPPER
Join B with sl st in first sc.

Rnd 1: Ch 2, hdc in each sc around; join with sl st in first hdc.

Rnd 2: Ch 2, hdc in each hdc to 1 st before toe marker, sk 1 st, hdc in marked st, sk next st, hdc in each hdc around; join with sl st in first hdc.

Rnd 3: Ch 2, hdc in each hdc to 3 sts before toe marker, sk 1 st, hdc in next st, sk 1 st, hdc in marked toe st, sk 1 st, hdc in next st, sk 1 st, hdc in each hdc around; join with sl st in first hdc.

Rnds 4 and 5: Ch 2, hdc in each hdc around; join with sl st in first hdc. Fasten off.

Rnd 6: Join A with sl st in first hdc, ch 1, sl st in each hdc around; join with sl st in first st.

Fasten off.

FINISHING
FLOWER
With C, ch 5; join with sl st in first ch to form a ring.

Rnd 1: (2 dc, sl st) in each ch (petal made) around – 5 petals. Fasten off.

FLOWER CENTER
With A, ch 3; join with sl st in first ch to form a ring.

Rnd 1: Ch 2, 3 hdc in ring. Fasten off, leaving a long tail for sewing. Layer flower, then center onto Slipper, sew in place through all thicknesses.

Weave in ends.

knit
STRIPED
booties

EASY +

Finished Sizes: 3-9 (9-12, 12-24) months
Foot Length: 3 (3½, 4)" [7.5 (9, 10) cm]

NOTE: Pattern is written for smallest size with changes for larger sizes in parentheses. When only one number is given, it applies to all sizes. To follow pattern more easily, circle all numbers pertaining to your size before beginning.

MATERIALS

LION BRAND® Vanna's Choice Worsted Weight
   yarn [3.5 ounces, 170 yards (100 grams,
   156 meters) per ball]

MEDIUM 4

   1 ball #173 Dusty Green (A)
   1 ball #109 Colonial Blue (B)
   1 ball #125 Taupe (C)
   1 ball #158 Mustard (D)
   or colors of your choice
LION BRAND Size 9 [5.5 mm] knitting needles or size
   needed for gauge
LION BRAND stitch markers
LION BRAND large-eyed blunt needle

GAUGE

16 sts and 22 rows = 4" [10 cm] in St st (k on RS, p on WS)
BE SURE TO CHECK YOUR GAUGE.

NOTE: Do not cut yarn between stripes. Carry yarn not in use along side of work.

BOOTIES (make 2)

With A, cast on 4 (6, 8) sts.

Work 2 rows in St st (k on RS, p on WS). With B, work 2 rows in St st. Repeat last 4 rows, AT THE SAME TIME, increase 1 st each end every 4th row twice – 8 (10, 12) sts.

Continue in stripe pattern until piece measures 3 (3½, 4)" [7.5 (9, 10) cm] from beginning. Mark each end of last row for fold line at toe. Work even in stripe pattern until piece measures 1½ (1¾, 2)" [4 (4.5, 5) cm] from markers, end with a WS row.

St. Jude patient Andy with Vanna

Volunteering is one of the most important things you can do. I encourage everyone to spend a little time with someone in need of attention and laughter. It will help you as much as it helps them.
—Vanna

SHAPE UPPER

Next Row: Work 4 (5, 6) sts, sl remaining 4 (5, 6) sts to holder. Work even in stripe pattern on 4 (5, 6) sts for first side until 3 (3½, 4)" [7.5 (9, 10) cm] above markers. Bind off.

Sl sts from holder back to needle, rejoin yarn and work second side same as first. Bind off. Inner edge of sides forms foot opening.

FINISHING

From RS, with A and beginning at left back edge, pick up and k 16 (18, 20) sts evenly spaced around edge of foot opening.

Beginning with a purl row, work in St st for 5 rows. Bind off.

Seam upper sides at center back for heel. Fold Bootie at markers, seam sole to upper.

Weave in ends.

knit
STRIPED GARTER STITCH slippers

Vanna during her visit at St. Jude

If you can find just a few minutes to give to your favorite charity, it will make a difference. Look around in your community. Someone needs your time.

—Vanna

●□□□ **BEGINNER**

Finished Sizes: Child's S (M, L)
Foot Length: 5 (6, 7) in. [12.5 (15, 18) cm]

NOTE: Pattern is written for smallest size with changes for larger sizes in parentheses. When only one number is given, it applies to all sizes. To follow pattern more easily, circle all numbers pertaining to your size before beginning.

MATERIALS
LION BRAND® Vanna's Choice Worsted Weight yarn [3.5 ounces, 170 yards (100 grams, 156 meters) per ball]
  1 ball #143 Antique Rose (A)
  1 ball #140 Dusty Rose (B)
  or colors of your choice
LION BRAND Size 9 [5.5 mm] knitting needles or size needed for gauge
LION BRAND Pom Pom maker
LION BRAND large-eyed blunt needle

MEDIUM 4

GAUGE
16 stitches and 32 rows = 4" [10 cm] in Garter stitch (knit every row)
BE SURE TO CHECK YOUR GAUGE.

NOTE: Do not cut yarn between stripes. Carry yarn not in use along side of work.

SLIPPERS (make 2)
With A, cast on 20 (24, 28) stitches. With A, knit 1 row. Change to B and knit 2 rows. Pick up A and knit 2 rows.
Repeat last 4 rows until piece measures 5 (6, 7)" [12.5 (15, 18) cm] from beginning, end with a wrong side row.
Last Row: (Knit 2 together) across row – 10 (12, 14) stitches. Cut yarns, leaving 10" [25.5 cm] long tails. Thread ends through remaining stitches. Pull tightly together and knot securely for toe.

FINISHING
Beginning at toe, sew edges together, working toward cast-on edge and leaving last 2¹⁄₂ (3, 3¹⁄₂)" [6.5 (7.5, 9) cm] open. Fold cast-on edge in half and sew together for heel.

POM POM (make 2)
Following package instructions, with A and B held together, make 2 small pom poms. Trim ends. Sew a pom pom to toe of each Slipper.

Weave in ends.

Knit Ribbed Hat instructions on page 58.

HATS & SCARVES

knit
DIVA scarf

EASY +

Finished Size: 10" x 42" (25.5 x 106.5 cm)

MATERIALS
LION BRAND® Vanna's Choice Worsted
Weight yarn [3.5 ounces, 170 yards
(100 grams, 156 meters) per ball]
1 ball #126 Chocolate (A)
1 ball #135 Rust (B)
1 ball #123 Beige (C)
1 ball #170 Pea Green (D)
or colors of your choice
LION BRAND knitting needles size 9 [5.5 mm]
or size needed for gauge
LION BRAND large-eyed blunt needle

ALTERNATE COLORS
LION BRAND® Vanna's Choice Worsted
Weight yarn [3.5 ounces, 170 yards
(100 grams, 156 meters) per ball]
1 ball #173 Dusty Green (A)
1 ball #140 Dusty Rose (B)
1 ball #170 Pea Green (C)
1 ball #143 Antique Rose (D)
or colors of your choice

ALTERNATE COLORS
LION BRAND® Vanna's Choice Worsted
Weight yarn [3.5 ounces, 170 yards
(100 grams, 156 meters) per ball]
1 ball #158 Mustard (A)
1 ball #140 Dusty Pink (B)
1 ball #099 Linen (C)
1 ball #142 Rose (D)
or colors of your choice

GAUGE
18 sts + 20 rows = 4" [10 cm]
in Pattern st
BE SURE TO CHECK YOUR
GAUGE.

PATTERN STITCH
(multiple of 12 + 6 sts)
Row 1: K3, *yo, k2tog; rep
from * to last 3 sts, k3.
Rows 2 and 4: K3, p to last 3
sts, k3.
Row 3: Knit.
Rows 5 and 8: K3, *k3tog,
k4, yo, k1, yo, k4; rep from *
across, end k3.
Rows 6, 7 and 9: K3, *p3tog,
p4, yo, p1, yo, p4; rep from *
across, end k3.
Rows 10-18: Rep Rows 1-9.
Rep Rows 1-18 for Pattern st.

SCARF
With A, cast on 42 sts. Work
Rows 1-8 of Pattern st.

Change to B and work Rows
1-18 of Pattern st.

Change to C and work Rows 1-18 of Pattern st.
Change to D and work Rows 1-18 of Pattern st.
*Change to A and work Rows 1-18 of Pattern st.
Change to B and work Rows 1-18 of Pattern st.
Change to C and work Rows 1-18 of Pattern st.
Change to D and work Rows 1-18 of Pattern st; Rep from * once more (12 stripes total).

Change to A and work Rows 1-8 of Pattern st for last stripe.

Bind off.

FINISHING
Weave in ends.

knit
striped
BOBBLE HAT

●■■■◻ **INTERMEDIATE**

Finished Sizes:
   Circumference: 18 (20, 22)" [45.5 (51, 56) cm]
   Height: 5³/4 (6³/4, 7¹/2)" [14.5 (17, 19) cm]

NOTE: Pattern is written for smallest size with changes for larger sizes in parentheses. When only one number is given, it applies to all sizes. To follow pattern more easily, circle all numbers pertaining to your size before beginning.

MATERIALS
   LION BRAND® Vanna's Choice Worsted **MEDIUM 4**
      Weight yarn [3.5 ounces, 170 yards (100 grams, 156 meters) per ball]
      1 ball #125 Taupe (A)
      1 ball #133 Brick (B)
      1 ball #158 Mustard (C)
      or colors of your choice
   LION BRAND Size 9 [5.5 mm] knitting needles or size needed for gauge
   LION BRAND split ring markers
   LION BRAND large-eyed blunt needle

GAUGE
16 sts and 32 rows = 4" [10 cm]
in Garter st
(k every row)
BE SURE TO CHECK YOUR GAUGE.

STITCH EXPLANATION
Make Bobble: K into front and back of next stitch twice, (turn, p4, turn, k4, turn) twice, (p2tog) twice, turn, k2tog. If Bobbles are worked from wrong side, push bobble to right side of work.

STRIPE SEQUENCE
*6 rows C, 2 rows B, 2 rows A, 2 rows C, 6 rows B, 2 rows A, 2 rows C, 2 rows B, 6 rows A, 2 rows C, 2 rows B, 2 rows A; rep from * for Stripe Sequence.

HAT
NOTE: Carry unused color(s) along edge of work.

BRIM
With A, cast on 72 (80, 88) sts.

Row 1 (RS): With B, k2, *make bobble, k3; rep from * to last 2 sts, make bobble, k1 – 18 (20, 22) bobbles.

Row 2: With B, knit.

Rows 3 and 4: With C, knit.

Rows 5 and 6: With A, knit.

Rows 7 and 8: With C, knit.

Rows 9 and 10: With B, knit.

CROWN

NOTE: Right and wrong sides of work reverse for crown of Hat.

Rows 1–7: With A, knit.

Work in Garter st (k every row), and Stripe Sequence until piece measures 3 (3$\frac{1}{2}$, 3$\frac{1}{2}$)" [7.5 (9, 9) cm] from beginning, end with a WS row.

Dec Row (RS): Maintaining Stripe Sequence, k1 (0, 2), *k12 (14, 15), k2tog, place marker; rep from * 4 more times, end k1 (0, 1) – 67 (75, 83) sts.

Next Row: Knit.

Next Row: *K to 2 sts before next marker, k2tog; rep from * 4 more times, end k 1 (0, 1).

Rep last 2 rows until 12 (10, 13) sts remain, end with a RS row.

Next Row: Knit, dec 2 (0, 3) sts evenly spaced across row – 10 sts.

Next Row (RS): *K1, make bobble; rep from * 4 more times.

Next Row (WS): K2tog across row – 5 sts. Cut yarn, leaving a long tail. Pull tail though remaining sts and knot.

FINISHING

Sew seam. Weave in ends.

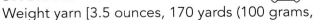 **EASY**

Finished Size: 9" x 60" (23 x 152.5 cm)

MATERIALS
LION BRAND® Vanna's Choice Worsted
Weight yarn [3.5 ounces, 170 yards (100 grams, 156 meters) per ball]
1 ball #170 Pea Green (A)
1 ball #130 Honey (B)
1 ball #174 Olive (C)
1 ball #126 Chocolate (D)
or colors of your choice
LION BRAND crochet hook size J-10 [6 mm] or size needed for gauge
LION BRAND large-eyed blunt needle

ALTERNATE COLORS
LION BRAND® Vanna's Choice Worsted
Weight yarn [3.5 ounces, 170 yards (100 grams, 156 meters) per ball]
1 ball #135 Rust (A)
1 ball #125 Taupe (B)
1 ball #108 Dusty Blue (C)
1 ball #109 Colonial Blue (D)
or colors of your choice

crochet
STRIPED
scarf

GAUGE
13 dc + 8 rows = 4" [10 cm]
BE SURE TO CHECK YOUR GAUGE.

NOTE: To change color, work last stitch to the point where there are 2 loops on hook, yarn over with new color to complete stitch.

COLOR SEQUENCE
*Work 1 row of A, 1 row of B, 1 row of C, 1 row of D; rep from * for Color Sequence.

SCARF
With A, ch 197.
Row 1: Dc in 3rd ch from hook (skipped ch-2 does not count as st), dc in each ch across; change to B in last st – 195 dc.
Row 2: Ch 2 (does not count as st), dc in each st across; change to C in last st.
Rep Row 2, following Color Sequence for a total of 15 rows, ending with C; change to D in last st. Do not fasten off.

EDGING
Rnd 1: With D, ch 2, turn, dc evenly spaced around all 4 sides of scarf, working 5 dc in each corner; join with slip st in top of first dc. Fasten off.

FINISHING
Weave in ends.

knit
SEED STITCH
hat

■■□□ **EASY**

Finished Sizes
Circumference: 16 (18, 20)" [40.5 (45.5, 51) cm]
Height: 6¹/₂ (7, 7¹/₂)" [16.5 (18, 19) cm]

NOTE: Pattern is written for smallest size with changes for larger sizes in parentheses. When only one number is given, it applies to all sizes. To follow pattern more easily, circle all numbers pertaining to your size before beginning.

MATERIALS
LION BRAND® Vanna's Choice Worsted Weight yarn [3.5 ounces, 170 yards (100 grams, 156 meters) per ball]
1 ball #140 Dusty Rose or #105 Silver Blue or color of your choice
LION BRAND Size 9 [5.5 mm] knitting needles or size needed for gauge
LION BRAND split ring markers
LION BRAND large-eyed blunt needle

GAUGE
16 sts and 22 rows = 4" [10 cm] in Seed st
BE SURE TO CHECK YOUR GAUGE.

PATTERN STITCH
Seed Stitch (even number of stitches)
Row 1 (RS): *K1, p1; rep from * across.
Row 2 (WS): *P1, k1; rep from * across.
Rep Rows 1 and 2 for Seed Stitch.

HAT
Cast on 64 (72, 80) sts. Work in Seed St until piece measures 2¹/₂ (3, 3¹/₂)" [6.5 (7.5, 9) cm] from beginning, end with a WS row.
Decrease Row (RS): *K6 (7, 8), k2tog, place marker; rep from * to end of row – 56 (64, 72) sts.
Next Row: Purl.
Next Row: *K to 2 sts before marker, k2tog; rep from * across.
Rep last 2 rows until 8 sts remain. Work even in Seed St for 4" [10 cm] for tie. Bind off.

FINISHING
Sew seam from lower edge of hat to bottom of Seed St tie. Knot tie at top of Hat. Weave in ends.

This wonderful young man is a joy to be around; his good spirits are an inspiration!

—Vanna

St. Jude patient Brett with Vanna

crochet
BERET

◼◼◻◻◻ **EASY**

Finished Size: Circumference: 20" (51 cm)

MATERIALS
LION BRAND® Vanna's Choice Worsted Weight yarn [3.5 ounces, 170 yards (100 grams, 156 meters) per ball]
1 ball #099 Linen or color of your choice
LION BRAND Size K-10.5 [6.5 mm] crochet hook or size needed for gauge
LION BRAND split ring markers
LION BRAND Pom Pom maker
LION BRAND large-eyed blunt needle

GAUGE
12 sc = 4" [10 cm]
BE SURE TO CHECK YOUR GAUGE.

BERET
Ch 6; join with sl st in first ch to form a ring.

Rnd 1: Ch 1, sc in each ch around; join with sl st in first sc – 6 sc.

Rnd 2: Ch 1, 2 sc in each sc around; join with sl st in first sc – 12 sc.

Rnd 3: Ch 1, *2 sc in next sc (inc made), sc in next sc; rep from * around; join with sl st in first sc – 18 sc.

Rnd 4: Ch 1, *2 sc in next sc, sc in next 2 sc; rep from * around; join with sl st in first sc – 24 sc.

Rnds 5-17: Rep Rnd 4, working one more sc after each inc – 102 sc at end of Rnd 17.

Rnds 18-20: Ch 2, hdc in each st around; join with sl st in first hdc.

Rnd 21: Ch 1, *sk next st (dec made), sc in next 16 hdc; rep from * around; join with sl st in first sc – 96 sc.

Rnd 22: Ch 1, *sk next st, sc in next 15 hdc; rep from * around; join with sl st in first sc – 90 sc.

Rnds 23-27: Rep Rnd 22, working one less sc after each dec – 60 sc at end of Rnd 27.

Rnd 28-30: Rep Rnds 18-20.

Fasten off.

FINISHING
POM POM
Following package instructions, make a medium pom pom. Trim ends. Sew to top of Beret.

Weave in ends.

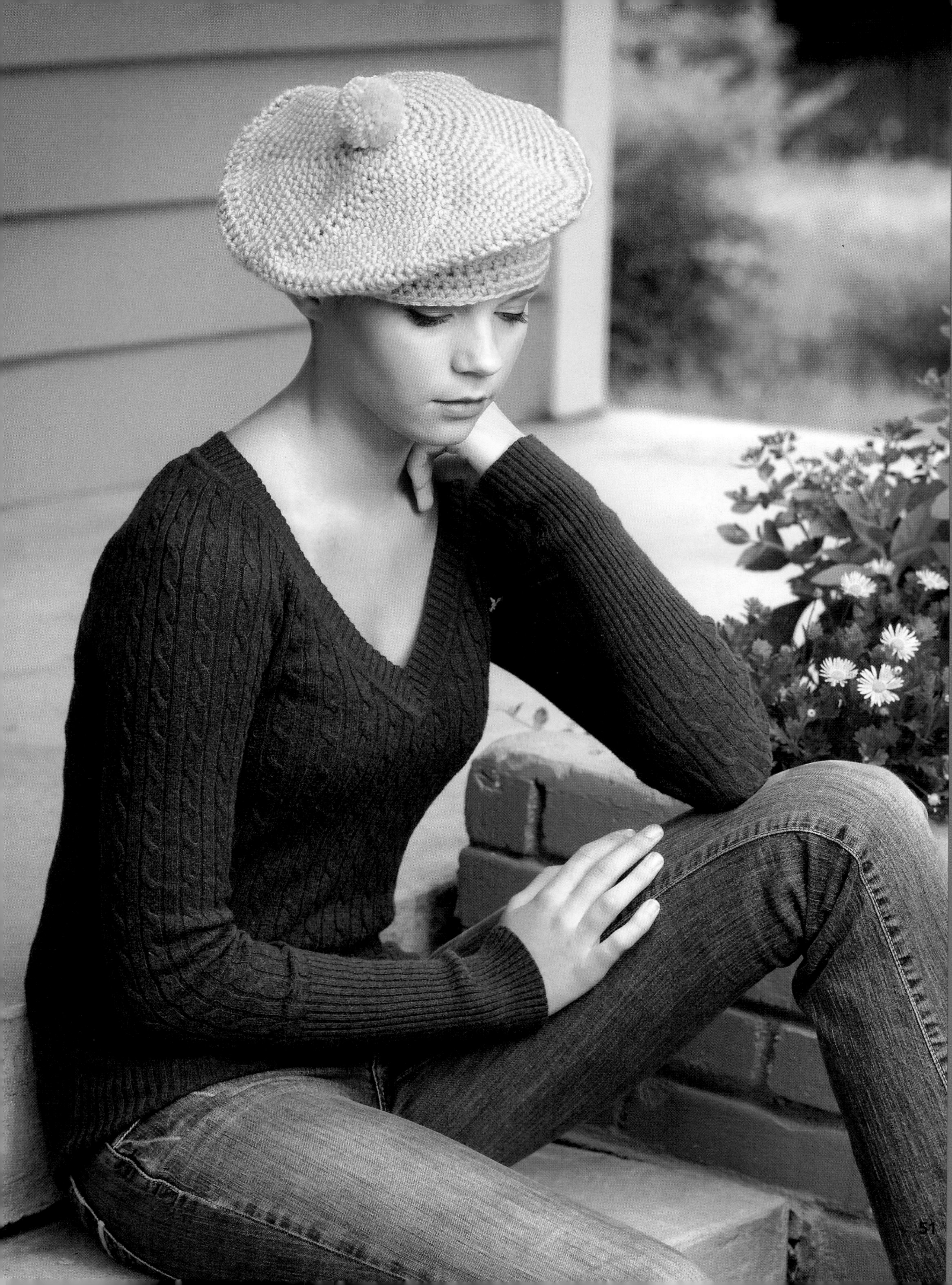

knit
JESTER hat

■□□□ **BEGINNER**

Finished Circumference: 18 (20, 22)" [45.5 (51, 56) cm]

NOTE: Pattern is written for smallest size with changes for larger sizes in parentheses. When only one number is given, it applies to all sizes. To follow pattern more easily, circle all numbers pertaining to your size before beginning.

MATERIALS

LION BRAND® Vanna's Choice Worsted Weight yarn [3.5 ounces, 170 yards (100 grams, 156 meters) per ball]
1 ball #109 Colonial Blue (A)
1 ball #170 Pea Green (B)
or colors of your choice
LION BRAND Size 9 [5.5 mm] knitting needles or size needed for gauge
LION BRAND Size 7 [4.5 mm] knitting needles
LION BRAND large-eyed blunt needle
5" [12.5 cm] piece of cardboard

GAUGE

16 stitches and 32 rows = 4" [10 cm] in Garter stitch (knit every row)
BE SURE TO CHECK YOUR GAUGE.

HAT
FRONT

With smaller needles and A, cast on 36 (40, 44) stitches.

Rows 1 and 2: With A, knit.

Change to B, but do not cut A. Carry color not in use up side of work.

Row 3: With B, knit.

Row 4: With B, purl.

Rows 5-8: Repeat Rows 1-4.

Rows 9 and 10: With A, knit.

Cut A. Change to larger needles and B.

Row 11: With B, knit.

Repeat Row 11 until piece measures 8 (8½, 9)" [20.5 (21.5, 23) cm]. Bind off.

BACK

Work as for Front, reversing colors.

FINISHING

Sew top and side seams.

TASSEL (make 2)

Wrap A and B around cardboard 40 times. Cut a piece of yarn 12" [30.5 cm] long and thread doubled onto large-eyed blunt needle. Insert needle under all strands at upper edge of cardboard. Pull tightly and knot securely near strands. Cut yarn loops at lower edge of cardboard. Cut a piece of yarn 12" [30.5 cm] long and wrap tightly 2-3 times around at top of tassel ${}^{1}/{}_{2}$" [1.5 cm] below top knot to form Tassel neck. Knot securely; thread ends onto needle and weave ends to center of Tassel. Trim Tassel ends evenly. Attach a Tassel to each top corner of Hat.

Weave in ends.

St. Jude patient Micah with Vanna

Listening to someone, whatever their age, is probably the best thing you can do for them.

—Vanna

crochet
POLKA DOT
hat

◼◼☐☐ **EASY**

Finished Circumference: 16" (41 cm)

MATERIALS

LION BRAND® Vanna's Choice Worsted Weight yarn [3.5 ounces, 170 yards (100 grams, 156 meters) per ball]
1 ball #170 Pea Green (A)
1 ball #109 Colonial Blue (B)
or colors of your choice

MEDIUM 4

LION BRAND Size K-10.5 [6.5 mm] crochet hook or size needed for gauge
LION BRAND Pom Pom maker
LION BRAND large-eyed blunt needle

ALTERNATE COLORS

LION BRAND® Vanna's Choice Worsted Weight yarn [3.5 ounces, 170 yards (100 grams, 156 meters) per ball]
1 ball #158 Mustard (A)
1 ball #133 Brick (B)
or colors of your choice

MEDIUM 4

GAUGE

12 hdc and 10 rows = 4" [10 cm]
BE SURE TO CHECK YOUR GAUGE.

HAT
BRIM

With A, ch 48; join with sl st in first ch to form a ring, being careful not to twist ch.

Rnd 1: Ch 2, hdc in each ch around; join with sl st in beg ch – 48 hdc.

Rnd 2: Ch 2, hdc in each hdc around; join with sl st in first hdc. Fasten off A. Join B with sl st.

MAIN SECTION

With B, rep Rnd 2 until piece measures 4" [10 cm] from beg.

SHAPE TOP

Rnd 1 (dec rnd): Ch 2, *hdc in each of next 7 hdc, sk 1 hdc (dec made); rep from * around; join with sl st in beg ch – 42 hdc.

Rnd 2: Ch 2, hdc in each hdc around; join with sl st in beg ch.

Rnd 3 (dec rnd): Ch 2, *hdc in each of next 6 hdc; sk 1 hdc; rep from * around; join with sl st in beg ch – 36 hdc.

Rnds 4-13: Rep last 2 rnds, working 1 less hdc between each dec – 6 hdc.

Fasten off, leaving a long tail. Weave tail through remaining 6 sts and pull tightly together. Fasten off.

Weave in end.

LARGE CIRCLE
(make 3)
With A, ch 6; join with sl st in first ch to form a ring.

Rnd 1: Ch 1, sc in each ch around; join with sl st in first sc – 6 sc.

Rnd 2: Ch 1, 2 sc in each sc around; join with sl st in first sc – 12 sc. Fasten off leaving a long tail for sewing.

SMALL CIRCLE
(make 3)
With A, ch 6; join with sl st in first ch to form a ring.

Rnd 1: Ch 1, sc in each ch around; join with sl st in first sc – 6 sc. Fasten off leaving a long tail for sewing.

FINISHING
From right side, sew circles as desired to Hat.

POM POM
Following package instructions, with A make a small pom pom. Trim ends. Sew pom pom to top of Hat.

Weave in ends.

crochet
GRANNY
SQUARE
hat

◧◼◻◻ **EASY**

Finished Circumference: 19" (48.5 cm)

MATERIALS

LION BRAND® Vanna's Choice [MEDIUM 4]
Worsted Weight yarn [3.5 ounces, 170
yards (100 grams, 156 meters) per ball]
1 ball #174 Olive (A)
1 ball #170 Pea Green (B)
1 ball #158 Mustard (C)
1 ball #109 Colonial Blue (D)
1 ball #147 Purple (E)
or colors of your choice
LION BRAND Size K-10.5 [6.5 mm] crochet
hook or size needed for gauge
LION BRAND Pom Pom maker
LION BRAND large-eyed blunt needle

GAUGE

Granny Square = 6½" x 6½" [16.5 x 16.5 cm]
BE SURE TO CHECK YOUR GAUGE.

HAT
GRANNY SQUARE (make 3)

With A, ch 4; join with sl st in first ch to
form a ring.

Rnd 1: Ch 3, 2 dc in ring, (ch 3, 3 dc in
ring) 3 times, ch 3; join with sl st in top
of beg ch. Fasten off.

Rnd 2: Join B with sl st in any ch-3 sp,
ch 3, (2 dc, ch 3, 3 dc) in same sp, *ch
1, (3 dc, ch 3, 3 dc) in next ch-3 sp; rep
from * 2 more times, ch 1; join with sl st
in top of beg ch. Fasten off.

Rnd 3: Join C with sl st in any ch-3 sp,
ch 3, (2 dc, ch 3, 3 dc) in same sp, *ch
1, 3 dc in next ch-1 sp, ch 1, (3 dc, ch 3,
3 dc) in next ch-3 sp; rep from * 2 more
times, ch 1, 3 dc in next ch-1 sp, ch 1;
join with sl st in top of beg ch. Fasten off.

Rnd 4: Join D with sl st in any ch-3 sp,
ch 3, (2 dc, ch 3, 3 dc) in same sp, *(ch
1, 3 dc in next ch-1 sp) twice, ch 1, (3
dc, ch 3, 3 dc) in next ch-3 sp; rep from *
2 more times, (ch 1, 3 dc in next ch-1 sp)
twice, ch 1; join with sl st in top of beg
ch. Do not fasten off.

Rnd 5: Ch 1, sc in each dc and ch-1 sp
around, working 3 sc in each corner ch-3
sp; join with sl st in first sc. Fasten off.

FINISHING

Sew Squares together to make a strip; sew ends of strip together to make a ring.

BRIM

Rnd 1: From right side, join A with sl st along one side of Granny Square ring; ch 2, work hdc evenly spaced around; join with sl st in first hdc. Fasten off.

Rep Rnd 1 with B, C, D and E.

At top of Hat, bring center point of each square together; sew together. Sew top edges of adjoining squares together through both thicknesses to form 3-corner top of Hat.

POM POMS

Following package instructions, make one pom pom each with A, B, and C. Trim ends. Sew a pom pom to each corner point at top of Hat.

Weave in ends.

Photo shown on page 43.

knit
RIBBED
hat

 EASY

Finished Size: Circumference 20" (51 cm)

MATERIALS

LION BRAND® Vanna's Choice **MEDIUM 4**
Worsted Weight yarn [3.5 ounces,
170 yards (100 grams, 156 meters)
per ball]
2 balls #143 Antique Rose
or color of your choice
LION BRAND Size 8 [5 mm] knitting
needles or size needed for gauge
LION BRAND large-eyed blunt needle
LION BRAND Pom Pom Maker

GAUGE

16 sts + 24 rows = 4" [10 cm] in k2, p2
Rib, slightly stretched
BE SURE TO CHECK YOUR GAUGE.

PATTERN STITCH

K2, p2 Rib
Row 1 (RS): *K2, p2; rep from * to last 2
sts, end k2.

Row 2: K the knit sts and p the purl sts.

Rep Row 2 for k2, p2 Rib.

HAT

Cast on 82 sts.

Work in k2, p2 Rib until Hat measures 7" (18 cm) from
beginning, end with a WS row.

Next Row (RS): K2, *p1, k1; rep from * to last 4 sts, p2tog,
k2 – 81 sts.

Next Row (WS): P2 *k1, p1; rep from * to last 3 sts, k1, p2.

Next Row: K2, *p1, k1; rep from * to last 3 sts, p1, k2.

Next Row: P2 *k1, p1; rep from * to last 3 sts, k1, p2.

Rep last 2 rows 2 more times.

SHAPE CROWN

Row 1 (RS): K2, p2tog, k the knit sts and p the purl sts to
last 4 sts, p2tog, k2 – 79 sts.

Rows 2-4: K the knit sts and p the purl sts.

Rows 5-80: Rep last 4 rows 19 times – 41 sts rem.

Row 81 (RS): K2, p2tog, k the knit sts and p the purl sts to
last 4 sts, p2tog, k2 – 39 sts.

Row 82 (WS): K the knit sts and p the purl sts.

Rows 83-114: Rep last 2 rows 16 times – 7 sts rem. Cut
yarn, leaving a long tail.

FINISHING

With large-eyed blunt needle, thread tail through rem sts
and pull tightly to secure. Sew seam.

Follow package instructions to make one large pom pom.
Sew pom pom to Hat.

Weave in ends.

GENERAL INSTRUCTIONS

ABBREVIATIONS

beg = begin(ning)
ch = chain
ch-sp = space previously made
cm = centimeters
dc = double crochet
dec = decrease
hdc = half double crochet
inc = increase
k = knit
k2tog = knit 2 together
k3tog = knit 3 together
mm = millimeters
p = purl
p2tog = purl 2 together
p3tog = purl 3 together
rem = remaining
rep(s) = repeat(s)
rnd(s) = round(s)
RS = right side
sc = single crochet
sk = skip
sl = slip
sl st = slip stitch
sp(s) = space(s)
st(s) = stitch(es)
t-ch = turning chain
tog = together
tr = treble crochet
WS = wrong side
yo = yarn over

* — When you see an asterisk used within a pattern row, the symbol indicates that later you will be told to repeat a portion of the instruction. Most often the instructions will say, repeat from * so many times.

( ) or [ ] — work enclosed instructions **as many** times as specified by the number immediately following **or** work all enclosed instructions in the stitch or space indicated **or** contains explanatory remarks.

GAUGE

Never underestimate the importance of gauge. Achieving the correct gauge assures that the finished size of your piece matches the finished size given in the pattern.

CHECKING YOUR GAUGE
CROCHET

Work a swatch that is at least 4" (10 cm) square. Use the suggested hook size and the number of stitches given. For example, the standard Lion Brand® Vanna's Choice gauge is: 12 single crochet + 15 rows = 4" (10 cm) on a size J-10 (6 mm) hook. If your swatch is larger than 4" (10 cm), you need to work it again using a smaller hook; if it is smaller than 4" (10 cm), try it with a larger hook. This might require a swatch or two to get the exact gauge given in the pattern.

KNIT

Work a swatch that is at least 4" (10 cm) square. Use the suggested needle size and the number of stitches given. For example, the standard Lion Brand® Vanna's Choice gauge is: 16 stitches + 22 rows = 4" (10 cm) on a size 9 (5.5 mm) needles. If your swatch is larger than 4" (10 cm), you need to work it again using smaller needles; if it is smaller than 4" (10 cm), try it with larger needles. This might require a swatch or two to get the exact gauge given in the pattern.

TERMS

continue in this way or as established — Once a pattern is set up (established), the instructions may tell you to continue in the same way.

fasten off — To end your piece, you need to simply pull the yarn through the last loop left on the needle. This keeps the last stitch intact and prevents the work from unraveling.

right side — Refers to the front of the piece.

work even — This is used to indicate an area worked as established without increasing or decreasing.

HINTS

Good finishing techniques make a big difference in the quality of the finished project. Do not tie knots. Always start a new skein at the beginning of a row or round, leaving yarn ends long enough to weave in later.

WHIPSTITCH

Place two Motifs, Squares, Blocks, or Strips with wrong sides together. Beginning in center of corner chs, sew through both pieces once to secure the beginning of the seam, leaving an ample yarn end to weave in later. Insert the needle from front to back through both loops on both pieces *(Fig. 1)*. Bring the needle around and insert it from front to back through next loops of both pieces. Continue in this manner, keeping the sewing yarn fairly loose.

Fig. 1

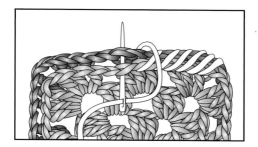

TASSEL

Cut a piece of cardboard 3" (3.75 cm) wide and as long as you want your finished tassel to be. Wind a double strand of yarn around the cardboard approximately 20 times. Cut an 18" (45.5 cm) length of yarn and insert it under all of the strands at the top of the cardboard; pull up tightly and tie securely. Leave the yarn ends long enough to attach the tassel. Cut the yarn at the opposite end of the cardboard (*Fig. 2*) and then remove it.

Fig. 2

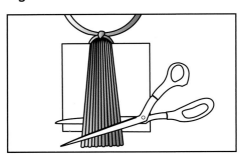

Wrap another length of yarn tightly around the tassel twice, ¹/₂" (12 mm) below the top (*Fig. 3*); tie securely. Trim the ends.

Fig. 3

BASIC CROCHET STITCHES & TECHNIQUES

CHAIN
(abbreviated ch)

To work a chain stitch, begin with a slip knot on the hook. Bring the yarn over hook from back to front, catching the yarn with the hook and turning the hook slightly toward you to keep the yarn from slipping off. Draw the yarn through the slip knot (*Fig. 4*).

Fig. 4

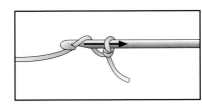

WORKING INTO THE CHAIN

Method 1: Insert hook into back ridge of each chain (*Fig. 5a*).
Method 2: Insert hook under top two strands of each chain (*Fig. 5b*).

Fig. 5a

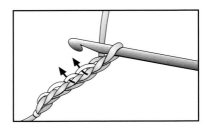

Fig. 5b

SLIP STITCH
(abbreviated slip st)

To work a slip stitch, insert hook in stitch indicated, yo and draw through st and through loop on hook (*Fig. 6*).

Fig. 6

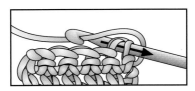

SINGLE CROCHET
(abbreviated sc)

Insert hook in stitch indicated, yo and pull up a loop, yo and draw through both loops on hook (*Fig. 7*).

Fig. 7

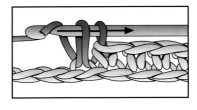

HALF DOUBLE CROCHET
(abbreviated hdc)

Yo, insert hook in stitch indicated, yo and pull up a loop, yo and draw through all 3 loops on hook (*Fig. 8*).

Fig. 8

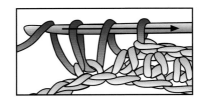

DOUBLE CROCHET
(abbreviated dc)
Yo, insert hook in stitch indicated, yo and pull up a loop (3 loops on hook), yo and draw through 2 loops on hook *(Fig. 9a)*, yo and draw through remaining 2 loops on hook *(Fig. 9b)*.

Fig. 9a

Fig. 9b

TREBLE CROCHET
(abbreviated tr)
Yo twice, insert hook in stitch indicated, yo and pull up a loop (4 loops on hook) *(Fig. 10a)*, (yo and draw through 2 loops on hook) 3 times *(Figs. 10b and 10c)*.

Fig. 10a

Fig. 10b

Fig. 10c

BACK OR FRONT LOOP ONLY
Work only in loop(s) indicated by arrow *(Fig. 11)*.

Fig. 11

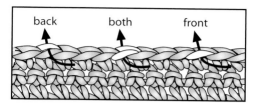

CHANGING COLORS
Work the last stitch to within one step of completion, hook new yarn *(Fig. 12)* and draw through all loops on hook.

Fig. 12

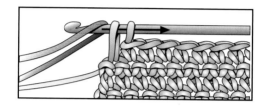

BASIC KNIT STITCHES & TECHNIQUES

SLINGSHOT CAST ON
Pull a length of yarn from the skein, allowing approximately 1" (2.5 cm) of yarn for each stitch to be cast on. Make a slip knot at the measured distance, pulling gently on both yarn ends to tighten the stitch on the needle. The yarn that comes from the skein is the **working yarn** and the other end is known as the **tail**. Hold the needle in your right hand with your index finger resting on the slip knot.

Place the short end of the yarn over your left thumb, and bring the working yarn up and over your left index finger. Grab both yarn ends with your other three fingers and hold them in your palm. There will be an upside down "V" of yarn between your thumb and index finger *(Fig. 13)*. (This is the "slingshot.")

Fig. 13

Insert the tip of the needle **under** the first strand of yarn on your left thumb *(Fig. 14)*.

Fig. 14

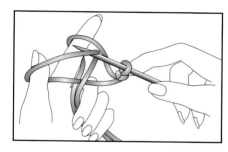

Bring the needle **over** and around the first strand on your index finger *(Fig. 15)*.

Fig. 15

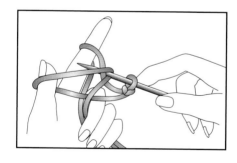

Pull the yarn and needle down through the loop on your thumb *(Fig. 16)*. The loop on the needle is your new stitch.

Fig. 16

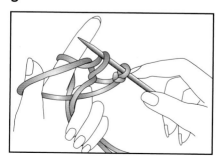

Slip your thumb out of the loop and bring it toward you, catching the yarn end to form a new loop on your thumb, and gently pulling to tighten the new stitch on the needle *(Fig. 17)*. Rest your index finger on the new stitch.

Fig. 17

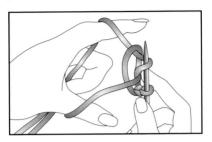

KNIT STITCH

Hold the needle with your cast on stitches in your left hand and pick up the empty needle with your right. Adjust the stitches so that the working yarn is hanging straight down from the first stitch.

With the working yarn away from you, slide the right needle from left to right into the stitch closest to the tip of the left needle *(Fig. 18)*.

Fig. 18

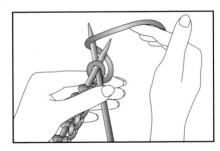

Hold the right needle between your left thumb and middle and index fingers and keep it under the left needle. Wrap the working yarn under the right needle. Then, bring the yarn between both of the needles and over the right needle *(Fig. 19)*.

Fig. 19

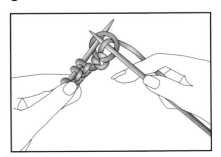

Take the right needle in your right hand. Bring the tip of the right needle out from under the left needle and through the stitch on the left needle, pulling the loop on the right needle toward you *(Fig. 20)*. Slip the old stitch off the left needle and tug on the working yarn to tighten the new stitch on the right needle.

Fig. 20

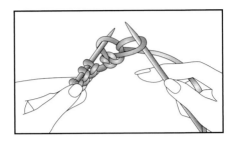

PURL STITCH

Start with the needle with the stitches in your left hand and the empty needle in your right. The working yarn should be hanging straight down from the first stitch.

With the working yarn closest to you, slide the right needle from right to left into the front of the first stitch *(Fig. 21)*.

Fig. 21

Hold the both needles between your left thumb and middle and index fingers. Going from right to left, wrap the yarn over the right needle and between both of the needles *(Fig. 22)*.

Fig. 22

Take the right needle in your right hand. Swing the tip of the right needle out from under the left needle and through the stitch on the left needle, pulling the loop on the right needle away from you *(Fig. 23)*. Slip the old stitch off the left needle and tug the working yarn slightly to tighten the new stitch on the right needle.

Fig. 23

BINDING OFF

Knit the first two stitches.

Use your left needle as a tool to lift the back stitch on the right needle up and over the front stitch *(Fig. 24a)* and completely off the right needle *(Fig. 24b)*. Don't forget to remove the left needle from the stitch.

Fig. 24a

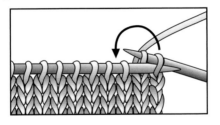

Fig. 24b

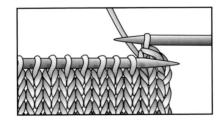

Knit the next stitch; you will have two stitches on your right needle. Bind off as before.

Continue until your left needle is empty and there is only one stitch left on your right needle.

Cut the yarn leaving a long end to hide later. Slip the stitch off the right needle, pull the end through the stitch (*Fig. 24c*) and tighten the stitch.

Fig. 24c

KNIT 2 STITCHES TOGETHER
(abbreviated K2 tog)

Insert the right needle into the front of the second, then the first stitch on the left needle as if to knit (*Fig. 25*) and knit them together as if they were one stitch. To knit 3 stitches together (K3 tog), insert the right needle into the third, then the second and first stitches on the left needle.

Fig. 25

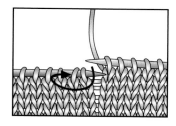

PURL 2 STITCHES TOGETHER
(abbreviated P2 tog)

Insert the right needle into the front of the first two stitches on the left needle as if to purl (*Fig. 26*) and purl them together as if they were one stitch. To purl 3 stitches together (P3 tog), insert the right needle into the front of the first three stitches on the left needle.

Fig. 26

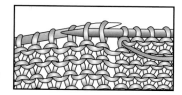

BAR INCREASE

This increase is also known as knitting into the front and the back of a stitch.

Knit the next stitch but do not slip it off the left needle (*Fig. 27a*). Instead, knit into the back of the same stitch (*Fig. 27b*), then slip it off the left needle.

Fig. 27a

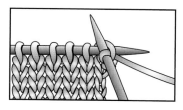

Fig. 27b

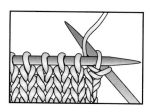

MAKE ONE
(abbreviated M1)

Insert the left needle under the horizontal strand between the stitches from the front (*Fig. 28a*). Then, knit into the back of the strand (*Fig. 28b*).

Fig. 28a

Fig. 28b

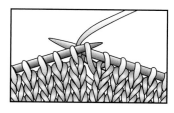

YARN OVER
(abbreviated YO)

Yarn overs are another method of increasing stitches. They form a hole in the fabric and are usually paired with a decrease to form lace patterns. Whatever stitch you need to make next after the yarn over determines where your yarn needs to be——in **front** for a purl or in **back** for a knit.

1. When a yarn over is between 2 knit stitches:
Bring the yarn forward between the needles, then back over the top of the right needle, so that the yarn is now in position to knit the next stitch (*Fig. 29*)

Fig. 29

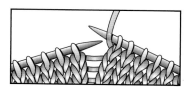

2. When a YO is after a knit stitch and the next stitch is a purl stitch:
Bring the yarn forward between the needles, then back over the top of the right needle and forward between the needles again, so that the yarn is now in position to purl the next stitch (*Fig. 30*).

Fig. 30

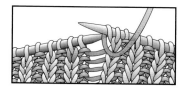

3. When a YO is between 2 purl stitches:
Take the yarn over the right needle to the back, then forward under the needle, so that the yarn is now in position to purl the next stitch (*Fig. 31*).

Fig. 31

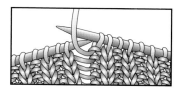

4. When a YO is after a purl stitch and the next stitch is a knit stitch:
Take the yarn over the right needle to the back, so that it is now in position to knit the next stitch (*Fig. 32*).

Fig. 32

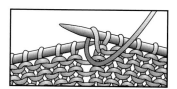

PICKING UP STITCHES KNITWISE

When instructed to pick up stitches, use one of the needles and the yarn that you are going to continue working with. Insert your knitting needle from the front to the back under two strands at the edge of the worked piece (*Figs. 33a & 33b*). Wrap the yarn around the needle as if to knit, then bring the needle with the yarn back through the stitch to the right side, resulting in a stitch on the needle.
Repeat this along the edge.

Fig. 33a (along the cast on or bind off edge)

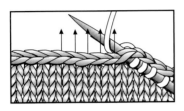

Fig. 33b (along the side edge)

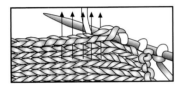

CABLES

There are many variations of cable patterns, but all are based on switching the position of stitches on your needle. Cables can twist to the right or to the left.
For a left-twisting cable or Front Cable: Work Row or Rnd as specified until you get to the Cable part; slip the indicated number of sts onto a cable needle as if to purl and hold them in **front** of your work. Knit the next number of indicated stitches on the left needle (usually the same number that is on the cable needle). Now, knit the sts from the cable needle onto your right needle, being sure that the first st you knit is the first one you slipped onto the cable needle, and finish the Row or Rnd.

To work a right-twisting cable or Back Cable, repeat the instructions, but hold the cable needle with the slipped stitches behind your work.

CHANGING COLORS

When changing colors, always pick up the new color yarn from beneath the dropped yarn and keep the color which has just been worked to the left (*Fig. 34*). This will avoid holes in the finished piece. Take extra care to keep your tension even.

Fig. 34

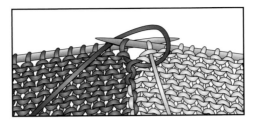

WEAVING — ONE STITCH IN

With the right side of both pieces facing you and edges even, sew through both sides once to secure the beginning of the seam. Pull the first and second stitches on the Front edge slightly apart. Notice the bars or horizontal strands between the stitches. Insert the needle under the bar between the first and second stitches on the first row and pull the yarn through (*Fig. 35*). Insert the needle under the next bar on the second side. Repeat, going from Front to Back, being careful to match rows. Repeat this process about six times on each side; pull your sewing yarn tightly and then stretch the seam gently. This helps to keep the seam as elastic as the knitting. Continue in this manner to the end of the seam, then weave in both yarn ends.

Fig. 35

Lion Brand Yarn Company
34 West 15th Street
New York, New York 10011
www.LionBrand.com

Leisure Arts would like to thank Baptist Health Medical Center, Little Rock, AR (www.Baptist-Health.com) for allowing us to photograph on their campus and Diamond Medical Equipment & Supply Inc. for the use of a wheelchai